ALIMA JALLOH-NORTH

MY AUTOBIOGRAPHY

TO

RICHARD

NICE MEETING YOU
@ THE CYCLIST EVENT
@ THE BIC
Alima JALLOH-NORTH
AJN

Disclaimer

This book is designed to provide information and motivation to our readers. It is sold with the understanding that the author and publisher are not engaged to render any type of psychological, legal, or any other kind of professional advice. The content is the sole expression and opinion of its author. Neither the publisher nor the individual author(s) shall be liable for any physical, psychological, emotional, financial, or commercial damages, including, but not limited to, special, incidental, consequential or other damages. Our views and rights are the same: You are responsible for your own choices, actions, and results.

The content of the book is solely written by the author.

DVG STAR Publishing are not liable for the content of the book.

Published by DVG STAR PUBLISHING

www.dvgstar.com

email us at info@dvgstar.com

DVG STAR
Dream ➤ *Vision* ➤ *Goal*
YOUR GOAL IS OUR MISSION

DEDICATION

This book is dedicated to my grandmother and mother who were the strong willed ladies in my life who taught me to be the lady I am today. As well as to my two beautiful children who I am thankful to GOD for making my world complete.

CONTENTS

ACKNOWLEDGMENTS

I would like to thank God for my parents, Mariama North and Michael Harold North, my stepfather for bringing me to England, and allowing me to study at a private boarding school in his home town. Thank you for all your love and support. And a special thank you to my father who came up with my book title, I am so grateful.

I feel so blessed to have had the privilege to be a mother, to my two brilliant children, Amza and Saffi, whom have taught me a lot about parenting, growing together, and allowing me to learn new things each day. You guys have brought so much joy into my life, the special bond we have as a triangle, love and respect for each other, unconditional love, plus a beautiful relationship. Your love and kindness, with the regular phone calls to help me with the technology, from which I am now almost an expert in. I really appreciate you, both and I love you very much.

My older brother, Mohamed Sultan Jalloh, you have been my rock, I thank you from the bottom of my heart. My entire life growing up together from our humble beginning in Freetown, I thank God to have been blessed with an amazing brother like you. You have helped me to write my book, with earlier recollection of our childhood. I love you and thank God for the special bond which has carried us throughout our lives.

My partner, Michael Antony McGowan, has been so supportive with my authors journey, you have come up with different ideas, titles, it has been such fun, always disturbing you, while you are watching your cycling race. But you never complained when interrupted by me. In the time I have been writing this book, I have not given you much attention but yet you continued to love and support me. Thank you for the happiness you have brought into me and my children's lives over the last six plus years. I love you to the moon and back.

Philip Chan, you have been a wonderful mentor to me. Always willing to give advice when asked, nothing is ever too much for you. Thank you for coming into my life, guiding, supporting and caring about me. You are a very special friend and I thank God for crossing our path.

Labosshy and Mayooran, thank you for all the fun, laughter and challenges we had endured during the last six to seven weeks. You have both been active listeners, given me new ideas and tips on how to write my story. I will never forget this experience as this has been one of the best in my life. All our conversations have always been so relaxing, sharing our knowledge, allowing me to express my extrovert ways of thinking, expressing my opinion during our telephone conversations, which I chose instead of the zoom, due to technical issues. Thank you for all your help, support and most of all your patience with me. I feel so blessed to have met you through Philip Chan last October 2018, at your DVG STAR event at the De Vere Grand Connaught Rooms in London. I appreciate all the hard work you and your team have done for me, with editing, formatting, publishing and the book cover design, which blew me away.

I definitely recommend DVG STAR, because they care about their authors. Thank you once again to you and your team of people for all your hard work, a job well done!!!! A very happy and satisfied customer, that's me indeed!!!

To all my friends, whom have given me some advice about my book, I would like to thank you all for your support.

FOREWORD

From her loving children.......

"I feel so privileged to have Alima as my mother. I am incredibly proud of all her achievements, leading up to and including this debut publication. As her daughter, I can honestly say that there is no one I know that is more genuine, loving and resilient than her. My mother's innate determination is something to be admired, and I hope that readers journeying through this book will learn from her as I did and discover just how truly special this wonderful lady is."

Lots of love,
Saffi xxx

"I grew up to be the person I was because of my mother. Her support of my ambitions and choices have and always will continue to push me further and further as I grow. Thank-you for everything Mama."

From Amza

There are only two certainties in life :
We are **BORN** and someday we will **LEAVE** this Earth and
in between it is up to us!

It is said that:

'A ship is safe in the harbour but this is not what it is designed to do!'

In this book, Alima wanted to show you why NOT taking
risks in life when opportunities present themselves could
mean you will be living an unfulfilled life! That was her case,
until one day, without hesitation, she said YES!

When you look beyond your horizon, you will start to
discover amazing things about yourself and opportunities,
just like the swallow flying across unknown lands and oceans
to discover richer grazing grounds.

When you look at some of the richest, most successful
people today and of the past. Many had situations in their
early life that was so unbearable beyond the imaginations of
"ordinary" people. Alima was the same. But Alima did not let
her circumstance shape her destiny but took actions to
change it however tough it was for a better life!

This is Alima's journey of transformation. She wants to
share with you and show you that there is light in your
moments of darkness. More than any one, you need to give
yourself the credit. YES YOU! **FACT DON'T COUNT!**

Alima's early life lacked what every child needs, namely,
the love from her parents. She was the first member of her
family to go to school. Often she was beaten badly by her
father. Her mother was working and consequently it was her
grandmother who attended to her. She saw so little of her
mother, it was age four before she knew the person bringing

her up was not her mother but her grandmother!

Later her parents got divorced, when she was 6 months old. Her parents brought her to Bournemouth, when she was a teenager.

For a long time she was working at low paid jobs until an opportunity to work for the NHS in 1991 gave her a better prospect. She married, had two beautiful kids, one boy and one girl but the marriage was dissolved in 2001 to cut a long story short, bringing up two kids was not easy as a single parent. Life is hard!

Richard Branson once said:

"When someone offers you an opportunity, say YES and work out the details later!"

Approximately 16 months before writing this book, a chance meeting with then a stranger, Sarah. They got talking in a supermarket and in due course became friends. Her friend Sarah, 7 months after their previous meeting invited her to come to a business meeting with her in London. Without a car and travelling by coach to London from Bournemouth would take hours!

This simple acceptance to say 'YES' was the start of her transformation and you will read more in her book of her autobiography.

This "meeting" was an invitation to the London Intelligent Millionaires Network, a business network where top 1% earners including millionaires and billionaires meet on a regular basis and other top Entrepreneurs from UK and abroad meet and learn from each other!

But I am just an ordinary person working in the NHS,

who am I to meet these people she thought to herself!

The key was that she said YES! We Humans often do one of three things: DELETE, DISTORT OR GENERALISE. They have their importance, however, HOW DO YOU KNOW WHAT YOU DON'T KNOW?

Read on in her autobiography and discover for yourself.

I want to wish you good reading but most of all TAKE ACTION because you are so much more than you think you are!

Philip Chan
10 Seconds Maths Expert
Multiple Awards Winning Author
Advisor to Government and Media

"Growing up with my wonderful sister, Alima, I saw greatness within her which she didn't see herself. She never got tired of doing little things for others, sometimes those little things occupied the biggest part of their hearts. She has such a personal characteristic that's so unique I guess only few people possess it, like doing good for others which is not a duty to her but she has got the joy of doing that. By bringing to the people that everything is possible in life.. The strongest weapon which is patience. Best security which is faith. Greatest tonic which is laughter and surprisingly she offers all this for free. Blessed to share the same DNA with this wonderful lady and loving sister."

Lots of Love
From Your Big Brother

"Make your life a masterpiece; imagine no limitations on what you can be, have or do."

~ Brian Tracy

CHAPTER 1
FREETOWN - SIERRA LEONE
WEST AFRICA

I was born in Cottage Hospital in Freetown, Sierra Leone, West Africa. This is my journey of survival, my journey of life's surprises, and about how I made a difference in other people's lives by sharing my story. Similar to a swallow I migrated from one place to another, and reflect the vibrant appearance of a swallow in my characteristic behaviour. I've always been a strong believer of being positive and full of smiles. Through my journey I have gone through hardship which has made me the independent and strong-minded woman I am today.

Sierra Leone was discovered by a Portuguese sailor, "Pedro da Sintra", in 1462. He discovered the Peninsula mountains while he was sailing the coast of West Africa. All the hills surrounding Freetown was called "Sierra Lyoa"

which means Lioness mountain. Freetown is the capital and largest city of Sierra Leone, which is known for its service for freed American slaves until about 1885. It was founded by British Naval Lieutenant John Clarkson. Freetown was part of the larger colony of Sierra Leone, which was founded by the Sierra Leone Company (SLC) in 1787. The beautiful town comprised of so much history going back to how they gained their independence in 1961. Even though it's such a beautiful town the lifestyle is, to say the least, for the local residents.

The Sierra Leone Creole People (or Krio people) is an authentic group in Sierra Leone, with some members having Native American ancestry as well. The vast majority of Creoles reside in Freetown and its surrounding western area. It is a major Port City on the Atlantic Ocean and is located in the western area of the country. Freetown is Sierra Leone's major urban, economic, financial, cultural, educational and political centre, as it is the seat of the Government of Sierra Leone.

The main minerals in Sierra Leone are diamonds, gold, iron, rutile and bauxite. The cotton tree is one of the oldest trees in Freetown and is in the centre of the city.

I remember as a child being taken to Lumley Beach on a Sunday afternoon. You can see the sun beaming away across the horizon. All the beaches on the Freetown Peninsula are some of the best in Africa. They have white sand backed by lush vegetation, with gentle azure waves. I could feel the gentle breeze rustling through my hair as I ran across the shore, taking in a breath of fresh air, the taste of the salty sea on the tips of my lips as I did so.

As a child, I was not allowed to go into the water, as I was told that it was "Mermmy Water". Tales were told to children that the mermaids liked to take children away. But I was happy that I could run across the sand and play with my friends.

It's a town filled with exotic beaches. There are five main beaches in Freetown which are definitely great for the tourists if you ever were to visit:

1. Lumley Beach
2. Tokeh Beach
3. Laka Beach
4. Radisson Beach
5. Bureh Beach

On Saturdays, my grandma would take us to Central Park, where they had a very large area for children to play on the swings, merry go-rounds and slides. It was a time in my life when I was carefree.

I didn't like ice cream as a child but I loved the local frozen yogurt they used to sell on the streets. They even sold coconut water, which was very refreshing during the day while it was hot. You could smell the freshness of the coconut when they slit the top and handed it over.

Weekends were a lot of fun, and I always tried to be good during the week so that our grandma could take us out to those places over the weekend as a treat. But sometimes I was a handful, as most little kids are. My favourite fruits were mango, avocado, and oranges. I preferred fish to meat and I still do.

Some of my favourite foods are a fundamental part of Sierra Leone cuisine, such as cassava leaves, which is the country's national dish. Stew is often served with jollof rice, white rice, plantains, yams, cassava and akar.

My Primary Carer, My Grandmother

My Grandmother

When my parents' marriage ended when I was a baby, we moved in with my grandmother, who was living in a single room on Gloucester Lane off Fourabay Road next to a latrine.

My grandmother, my mother, my older brother, Mohamed, and I lived in that single room for a few years. I slept on the floor with my brother, while my grandmother and mother slept on the bed.

My mother faced a lot of struggles. She couldn't be there

for us, as she had to earn money to be able to provide food and shelter. She used to go into different parts of town trading. As my mother was not around our grandmother became the primary carer for my brother and I.

My grandmother was 5ft tall, and she had a large gap between her teeth. She was a kind, loving, caring and compassionate lady who was my world. She had a child-like voice, which I found amusing when I was growing up in Freetown. She also wore our traditional clothing and her favourite colours were green, red, white and blue. Our traditional clothing, which is called "docett-en-lappa" in Creole, which means a long wrapper around the waist down to the floor, then a loose kaftan-like-top, with a headscarf, and flip-flops. She did not own any shoes. She was a very content, prayerful and Godly woman. She gave my older brother and me the gift of hope and encouragement in our difficult times. Jaja, as we use to call her, was so thoughtful and generous when she stepped in to look after us, permanently, when I was at a very tender age of 6 months old and my older brother was only 2 years old.

My grandmother made my brother and I feel loved, valued and special. My brother and I were the first generation to be educated. I feel so blessed to have had the privilege to have been educated. Even though my grandmother was illiterate, she was gifted with wisdom and was good with her mental maths. Our home was a happy and safe haven, even though we were too young to understand what our circumstances were.

Every morning my grandmother would wake up before 05.00 am to pray and never went back to sleep. I could hear her praying for my brother and me on a daily basis. She would get my brother and I ready for school. We walked about 10 minutes to the mixed primary school, called "Amadiya Primary School", on Gorie Street From our first floor flat in Mountain Court which my mother and stepfather rented for us. We lived in the east end of Freetown, which was the rough end of town. The crime rate was high, with burglaries, gambling, fighting in the streets, youth problems, drunkenness, drugs, and worst of all, poverty. After seeing all these things happening around me as a child, while I was growing up, I knew at that tender age that I will never drink, smoke or take any substance and have never done so in my entire life!

I remember moving to Mountain Court when I was about four years old. I was so excited that we were going to live in a concrete building, and my brother and I were going to have our own bedroom. Also I loved the idea of a first floor flat with a set of stairs. The veranda was amazing; when I was standing there I could see the top of my road, which had a slight slope. At the back of the house were hills and mountains, giving us such a scenic view that I had never experienced before.

The compound we lived in was a concrete house with a front-facing veranda, which was converted into a ground floor flat with three bedrooms and a lounge. The first floor flat also had three bedrooms and a lounge. We only occupied two bedrooms, the third bedroom was kept by the Landlady, Mamie Tejan, who owned the property but lived outside the city and only used to visit three to four times a year. Her nephew lived in Freetown and he came and collected the rent at the end of each month.

The house was facing the main Mountain Court. At the rear of the house, there were three separate concrete bungalow-like stones and two sets of concrete stairs on either side of the building. One was a separate one-bedroom flat, and the other was a two-room flat with a small lounge, plus two separate studios. At the back of the compound was another concrete building which was a studio flat, and next to it was the only tap that supplied water for everyone. On the right of the studio was the kitchen where everyone did their cooking. On the left side by the tap was the shower room, which had a crown like look. When you turned the tap head clockwise it opened, and when your turned it anti-clockwise, it switched off. Next to the shower room was the latrine, which was a very deep hole with a wooden square to sit on. Both the shower room and the toilet had a wooden door with a latch on. In the kitchen area, there were good sized stones, and you put firewood between the stones and then put the cooking pot on top. There were four cooking sets of stones in the kitchen, which meant you could not have more than four families at a time in the kitchen, cooking. There were twenty-one people living in that compound.

As an inquisitive young child, my grandmother embraced my personality and wanted her generation to be last, to be submissive and be the silent generation. The adults in our compound and neighbourhood could not understand why my grandmother was allowing me to grow up as an extroverted little girl who asked lots of questions. It was my grandmother who raised my brother and I for the majority of our childhood, and she acted as my first female role model. In a time where little girls were expected to be meek and demure, my natural curiosity was typically perceived as an impertinence. I was often labelled as a "difficult child". However, instead of chastising me, my grandmother nurtured the inquisitive child in her care and made me feel safe, loved and confident enough to embrace the best parts of myself and strive towards my dreams. She challenged traditions and encouraged me to develop my own voice, and did not let cultural barriers stand in my way. These values carried me through the various milestones and challenges I would experience later in my life.

We didn't have any real toys; my brother and I were creative, so we used to use cardboard boxes and empty tins to make our own toys. We made a phone, different animals and so on. I used to love the rainy season, as we were allowed to play in the rain on our streets with the other kids, it was so much fun. There were gutters on one side of the road just outside our house where all the water poured through. They were not like ordinary gutters; they were made purely out of cement. During the rainy seasons it became a mini river as we lived on the slopes of the mountain side. It was a mesmerising view and an unforgettable sight when all the children splashed across the puddles on the street. Those were the few happy and special moments in my life.

In the evenings I would sit with my grandmother, who used to tell me stories about her childhood with her parents. She had many brothers and she was the only girl. That was where she learnt at an early age how to be a strong woman.

After school, my brother and I would carry a tray of cola-nuts on our heads to sell for a few hours on the street, but we were only allowed to go as far as within our neighbourhood. My grandmother also had a tray of cola- nuts outside our house, and people in our neighbourhood and the surrounding area would usually buy cola-nuts from us.

It's been such a blessing to know that we were the first generation to be educated, such a privilege. I thank God for having that privilege to have been able to have such a solid foundation at an early age, which has helped me to become the woman I am today.

Just over a year old
in Gloucester Lane,
Freetown

At the age of 2 years old

Freetown, 1975s

Freetown, 1980s

"We Generate Fears While We Sit. We Overcome Them By Action."

~ Dr. Henry Link

CHAPTER 2
YEARNING FOR MORE

LIVING WITH MY FATHER IN MOYAMBA

This was the time I decided to go live with my father in Moyamba District, in the Southern Province of Sierra Leone. It is the largest city in the Southern Province of Sierra Leone. The first president of Sierra Leone, Saika Stevens, was born in Moyamba. The main language is Mende, but there are other languages spoken.

Me, In Moyamba

I went because my older brother had already been living with him for a year and felt that I had an empty space inside of me which I yearned for a father figure to fill. Of course my grandmother and mother looked after me well; nonetheless there was a part of me which wanted to get to know my father better and to have him play a role in my life and upbringing. How wrong could I have been?! This part of my life spiralled out of control and left me with scars which to this day haunt me from the stories I'm about to tell.

My journey on the 21st of September 1975, a bright and sunny day even though it was the rainy season, was surely

17

very insightful. My grandmother had given me two Leones as pocket money for my journey. I travelled unaccompanied but felt safe at the same time. I was the only child on the coach. I was mesmerised by how brave I was at that tender age.

I thoroughly enjoyed the scenery during the journey. I saw many villages and children chasing the coach, laughing and smiling, they looked so content and happy. Their grandparents were sitting on their verandas, watching the world go by. I could see their grey hair from a distance. It is a tradition for families to live together, especially within village life. I imagined being one of those children, having that lifestyle, surrounded by all my family, filled with play and laughter. It's a dream for any child to be loved, nurtured and to be cared for unconditionally.

I hardly spoke to anyone, as I didn't want to miss out on any aspect of my journey. All I could keep on thinking about was what my dad's house looked like and was hoping that I would be able to have my own bedroom for the first time in my life.

The coach made three stops. The first stop was at Waterloo, where I bought some cassava bread, a famous snack which was popular at that time. The second coach stop was at MILE 91, where I bought some Aboubour, which is bread with beans and fish cooked together, with a cold Pepsi. The third stop before the final destination was Moyamba Junction. I got out of the coach to stretch my legs and looked around. Lots of people got off at this stop to connect to their destination, while other people boarded the coach. When I boarded the coach this time, an elderly lady sat next to me and was going to Moyamba Town, and she also happened to know my father because our house was only four doors away from hers. I could hardly believe what I was hearing.

As a local, born and bred of that town, I started to ask her so many questions about the town, eagerly wanting to know more before we reached our final destination stop.

My father and older brother met me at the coach station which was less than a minute and a half from my dad's bungalow. I was so excited to see them both. My eyes lit up and I ran into my father's arms to embrace his love and to show him how much I had missed his presence in my life.

After arriving at the property I was shown my own room, which was facing the main road. I had a double bed and a large bedroom, about fourteen by fourteen square feet, a square-shaped room. I had my own indoor bathroom and a separate toilet.

The bungalow had four bedrooms with a veranda. The front door was in the middle of the bungalow with a glass-panel which led into the main lounge. The dining area was part of the lounge, an open-plan. There were two bedrooms and a bathroom in the middle with a separate bathroom and separate toilet on either side of the bungalow

Only my father, my older brother and my cousin, who was visiting at the time, were living in the bungalow. I went up to the telephone exchange to send a cable message to my grandmother's neighbour to tell her that I had arrived safely at my father's place.

The Arrival of the Monster from Hell

Life was pretty great with just my father as I got the love I yearned for from my father. A few months later my whole world turned upside down with the arrival of my stepmother. You may be wondering where this character had come from. My father remarried but due to unresolved issues between them they had separated for a few months while she went to live with her relatives. But now she was back and this is when my nightmare began!

My stepmother arrived, with my half-sister who was about four at the time and my half-brother was just over a year old.

My biggest nightmare started upon her arrival in that bungalow. The first thing she said to me was, "If you think by coming to stay with your father, your mum will come and reconcile with him, then think again!"

My mother had already been married to my stepfather by then so surely I thought nothing of the sort. They had two children, my younger sister, Jennifer, and my brother Andrew. Jenny was almost four years old, while Andrew was just under one year old. They were happily married, and to be honest she had nothing to worry about. I personally though it was her insecurities that led her to feel that way, and she thought that we were going to get in the way of her living with my father. Yet deep down she was jealous of us and the love our father was showering on us.

Within 24 hours of my step-mother arriving in Moyamba, she started to tell my older brother and me off for no reason, shouting and screaming at us, always telling us to clean, sweep, mop and to even do the gardening. This would have been fine if it was asked out of love, as children do need to help around the house. But this was her merely trying to use us as slaves.

I refused to do any work, as I was not used to doing any housework when I lived with my grandmother. Whenever I refused my step-mother would reach out for the cane to flog me. With all her maximum adult strength she would beat me until my body and face were so bruised that I could hardly recognise myself. The bruises were so raw and sore for days and weeks on end. I had been warned not to make any noise, so that our neighbours wouldn't hear us in pain.

When my father returned home from work, he could see that I had been beaten but he wouldn't say anything. I realised then that she was the one wearing the trousers in that marriage.

It made me so sad that my own father could consciously watch his children getting beaten up and not say a single word to keep it from happening and to comfort us from the pain we endured. My older brother was also beaten in the same aggressive manner. We both comforted each other.

We were so traumatised by the way she was treating us that it felt like it became the norm of everyday life. There were times when she would hardly give us food after cooking a feast for her children. She only gave us the rice at the bottom of the cooking pot, with the oil from the under-side of the palm-oil-bottle.

My stepmother, my father, and my younger brother and sister would sit at the dining table, while my brother and I served them. They would eat until their stomachs were full, while my older brother and I were their unpaid servants. We were only allowed to eat after we had washed all the dishes and finished the cleaning, and yet this would be a very tiny meal that just kept us barely alive.

Since her arrival, our father suddenly stopped all communications with us. Everything changed in that home. It was as if we no longer were his children but merely slaves who worked for them.

The worst part was, our father started beating us up as well nearly every single day. This was the side I had never seen in him until then. My dreams of coming to live with a loving father were shattered into pieces. It was as if I had entered my worst nightmare and couldn't wake up from it. I couldn't understand why this was happening to me. Was it too much to want a father who loved us, to want to nurtured and cared for, to want to live a life where we could stay as a happy family, just like the children I saw playing outside on my route to Moyamba? If it weren't for my brother I would have felt so isolated with no one to share my pain. The only reassurance for me was having him.

At St Joseph's Primary School, Moyamba

I started at St Joseph's Primary School in September of that year. My teachers were very concerned about my physical injuries and wanted to report my parents to the police. But I was afraid that I would get more beatings at home if my school got involved with my family issues. My brother's school also wanted to report them to the police, but we were frightened of what the outcome would be.

Each day my older brother and I would wake up at 06.00am and do all the housework, cleaning and polishing, before we got ready for school. Then we both walked to and from school each day. We were the ones who had to go collect water in big buckets and carry them back on our heads. The clothes we wore were all second-hand as our step-mother refused to buy us new clothes. The days were long and I became weak day by day from the torture I was being put through. This is not how a child's life should be, why was this happening to me? Every day I wished it was just a nightmare that I would wake up from but it never was. Even servants had days off from their duties but we were treated like slaves. I felt like we were actually living the fairy tale of Cinderella. If only I could have been whisked away.

I enjoyed being at school, at least I only got a smack on

my hand when some of the girls were causing problems in the class, which was less painful than the daily beating I received from my step-mother and father. Those days, schools were allowed to smack children to discipline them.

One night, my brother and I were very hungry, we waited for our parents to go to sleep before we sneaked into the bedroom next to their room where the fridge was kept. While my brother was checking that no one was awake and was being the look out, I went to raid the fridge. I felt like a burglar in my own home stealing food, which my brother and I shared. We were prepared for the penalty the following morning.

The next morning at the break of dawn I could hear my father screaming my name to come to him. When I got there, he was fuming with anger. The bathtub was half-full, and he ordered me to get into the bath, which I did, fully clothed. He then took off the belt he was wearing and started to beat me up. With all his force he began beating me all over. I could feel the rough texture of the belt against my skin and the sound of the belt as he beat me non-stop. I cried silently, pleading with him to stop beating me. I had been told not to shout a few months ago to ensure that the neighbours didn't hear my screams. Then my father called my older brother and also told him to get into the bathtub. My stepmother walked in and began beating him. The life we lived was brutal, and to this day it has haunted me and the scars remain all over my body as proof of the torture we went through.

We could not believe how our daily lives had become a nightmare since our step-mother arrived. I was very cheeky and verbal with the grown-ups. I did not care anymore, as I got so used to being beaten up, I stopped feeling pain. With all the abuse, I still hoped that my father would change and start to love my brother and I as he did before she arrived.

We told our mother and grandmother about what was going on yet we continued to stay with our father, which was our choice. I was shocked to find out that my grandmother said she already knew about the beating as it had happened to my brother before. But she didn't stop me from going, as she felt it was not her place to say, and me being a stubborn child back then wouldn't have believed her and would have gone anyway despite what she said or thought.

Eventually I passed my 11-plus exams. My mother was eager to get me away from my father after finding out what was happening to me so she paid for me to attend St Joseph's Secondary School in Moyamba which was a boarding school. By this time, my father was transferred to another town with his new job. My brother continued to stay with him, which was his own choice.

I was very excited to attend an all-girls boarding school in Moyamba. I was scared for many years after living in my father's home. I was no longer that happy child that left Freetown a few years before. This caused lots of issues throughout my teenage and adult years. I learnt not to get too attached to people, and had a problem with trusting them.

However, in 1991 my father, wrote a letter from Freetown,

apologising about everything that had happened in Moyamba from 1975, while my older brother and I were staying with him. The letters were an Air Mail Letters, which I have kept up to this day. My older brother and I forgave our father, and moved on.

As I grew up...

"Security Is Mostly A Superstition. Life Is Either A Daring Adventure Or Nothing."

~ Helen Keller

CHAPTER 3
A WHOLE DIFFERENT WORLD

Family portrait
(My stepfather, mother and siblings)

My stepfather came to Sierra Leone in the late sixties. This is when he met my mother in Kono in 1969. At the time I was only four years old. He was working for a mining company, SLST "Sierra Leone Selection Limited", in Yengema, Eastern Province of Sierra Leone. My mother was a trader at that time, travelling across Sierra Leone. A friend of hers invited her to a dinner-dance ball, and this is where she met my stepfather and they both fell in love.

Within three months of getting to know each other they got married, and they've been with each other ever since. My mother and my stepfather have a daughter called Jennifer and a son called Andrew. They are my half-sister and brother. Both Jennifer and Andrew were born in Freetown, and they spent the first few years of their lives in Freetown.

When my step-father got the job with Aramco in 1975, he was living in a one bedroom flat, then got transferred to North Camp, which was a three bedroom trailer or commonly known as a caravan home. My mum, half sister and brother lived with him. My siblings attended an America School. Few years later the family moved to Salamia Avenue, at the Dhahran Compound.

Photos from our house in Salamia Avenue

My stepfather had a place in Bournemouth, Dorset, in the UK which is where they often travelled for their summer holidays. It was a beautiful place surrounded by the waves of the beach.

My mother and I in Bournemouth

One day my mother decided that it was time I visited Bournemouth. She travelled to Freetown to bring me to Bournemouth. By then, Jennifer and Andrew had already migrated to live in Bournemouth with their grandmother, my stepfather's mother, known as Granny North. My stepfather stayed with my younger brother and sister. Mother made all the necessary arrangements from St Joseph's Secondary School in Freetown, which I was attending at that time.

Summer of 1982

I arrived in Bournemouth in the middle of July 1982. When mother and I arrived at Gatwick Airport, my step-father, Jennifer and Andrew met us at the airport. It was a funny feeling. As I walked through the airport gates, it sunk into me that I had officially left Freetown. It was a new adventure awaiting me outside those gates, a new life, a new beginning. At that time I hadn't realised I wouldn't be going back to Freetown.

We walked to the large caravan my stepfather had hired for that summer, so that we could travel across the UK during the six week summer holiday.

I originally came to England for a short holiday, as I had a return ticket back to Freetown. But after everything that happened with my father, my mother decided it was better for me to stay in Bournemouth.

She needed me to start school in Bournemouth, so she did her research and I eventually joined the St Mary's Gate

School in Southbourne, Bournemouth, which was a small private school for girls. The buildings were Victorian style, with black and white paint at the front.

Bournemouth Pier

The pier is located in the town centre in one of the most popular seaside towns in the South West. With its long sandy beach, it's a great place to surf. People come from all over the world to visit this beautiful town which has so much to offer to the public. It has a great night life with so much to do in the area. Being a typical tourist town, Bournemouth is a small town in the County of Dorset, which is in the South of England. Bournemouth was also famous for having lots of hotels and bed and breakfasts in the 1980s. There are few large department stores, like Debenhams, House of Frazer, and Beals. These are household names. The town centre has different kinds of shops: clothes shops, boutiques on Westover Road, and an ice rink where I used to do ice skating as a teenager with my friends. There is also The Pavillion Theatre which hosted nearly all the shows in town. It also has a massive ballroom next to the theatre, and this building has been around since the 1920s. The style of the building is Victorian. It can seat at least 1500 people. The stage is huge, with the ballroom dance floor being very spacious. The theatre is very busy all year round. I have attended many functions there over the years. The local buses in Bournemouth are yellow. The Royal Bath Hotel is supposed to be one of the first hotels in this town, and it's located next to Bournemouth Pier, on the right. The building is Victorian, with incredible décor and large corridors with a massive lounge and dining area.

I worked as a waitress in this hotel. The kitchen is situated down a slope, which has couple of steps to climb up before getting into the restaurant. When I worked there, the silver service dishes were quite heavy, with 12 to 14 portions of red or white meat, which was served by me. Trying to get between guests siting at the table was awkward, but I still managed to do my part time job. It was a miracle that nobody ever fell or slipped on those stairs during my shift. Another waiter would follow behind me, serving the vegetables and potatoes. I worked for an agency during that time, which meant I had the chance to go to different hotels. I enjoyed this, as it gave me people skills, communication and helped me learn to deal with difficult customers. I also worked as a chambermaid when there were no waitressing jobs available. The agency was a small office up the Triangle, which was next to the post office.

The beach has lots of beach-huts, and they are brightly painted with different colours. Some are owned privately by people, while others are rented out during the summer sea peak tourist season. People would usually spend most of their day in their beach huts, watching the world go by, swimming, reading, surfing, and spending quality time with their families or loved ones.

There is also Boscombe Beach, which is on the far left of Bournemouth Pier. Boscombe is famous for its weekly market, lots of small shops run by families, cafes, pubs, hair dressers, news agents, and the Chiropractor College plus many attic shops on the high street towards Pokesdown.

Further from Pokesdown is Turton, then Christchurch a few miles down the coast from Bournemouth. Christchurch has beautiful countryside, the New Forest, with small country lanes, many horses, large country manors, and Mores Valley, which is very popular for picnic and day trips. Christchurch has the largest popular of pensioners in England. Again, it's because of the warmer climate in this county of Dorset. There are lots of shops on the high street with cafés, a post office, a pharmacy, a supermarket, restaurants, hotels, pubs and parks. Highcliffe is next to Christchurch. Also, the Priory is in Christchurch, just off the main high street, by the Avon River. The Priory is supposed to be one of the longest Parish Churches in England. The building is like no other, a real masterpiece of its kind. There is also Highcliffe Castle, another old and superb building surrounded by an amazing landscape, which leads to a beach of its own with a zigzag slope.

Bournemouth has the highest population of pensioners in England, with lots of nursing homes. It is known for its brilliant warmer weather all year round, compared to the rest of England.

On the right of Bournemouth Pier in the Bournemouth International Centre (BIC) there is Westcliff, full of many hotels, B&Bs, restaurants, cafés, supermarkets, and small shops. The Highcliffe Hotel is almost next door. There is an arcade in Westbourne, which is almost in the middle of the shopping high street. There are small shops and an old-fashioned hardware shop. There are many more shops on the main high street, as well as cafés, restaurants, pharmacies a bingo hall, a collection of boutiques and a post office.

Cultural Differences

I had to get used to the difference in cultures between being in Sierra Leone and Bournemouth. There was so much difference in the way people lived their lives. The lifestyle was very different. Even though it was such a big change I was able to adapt.

When I arrived in Bournemouth in 1982, it was just a small and quiet town. There were very few ethnic minorities living there. I did not know any other black teenagers. I think my school had about nine black girls who arrived at different times, including a few mixed race girls. I did not personally experience any racial discrimination at St Mary's Gate. I was happy to be in boarding school, which had many challenges of its own, but I kept on going and worked very hard at school. All the teachers were supportive, especially my favourite French teacher Madam Khan. I never really settled into the way of life but I carried on, because when you are a child, you sometimes have to do things that are in your parents' best interest. There was nothing I could have done about my circumstances. Having been to boarding school from the age of eleven, my whole life was kind of sheltered in a way.

After I left school, my parents were still working for Aramco in Dhahran, Saudi Arabia. I stayed in our family home, house-sitting. My parents travelled to England in the summer, and my mother would also visit Freetown, Sierra Leone to visit her mother, my grandmother.

I remember my first visit back to Freetown in 1988. I was so excited for Christmas as I was going to see my grandmother and my other relatives. My grandmother was so surprised to see how much I had grown and matured within the six years since I left Freetown. By this time she had other health issues and looked older than when I last saw her. I felt sad for her. She told me that after I had left Freetown in 1982, she felt empty, and when my older brother left in 1984, she didn't know what to do with herself. I suppose we were her life. The weather was warm and humid in Freetown, and the three-week holiday went ever so quickly. We went to the beach nearly every day like old times, and met other holiday makers too. Then it was time to return to Bournemouth.

My Grandmother and I, in Freetown when I returned.

This photo was taken in 1989 while I was on holiday in Freetown with my elder brother Mohamed

"The Only Limit To Our Realisation Of Tomorrow Will Be Our Doubts Of Today."

~ Franklin D. Roosevelt

CHAPTER 4
BOARDING SCHOOL

My mother chose St Mary's Gate School (SMG) on Belle Vue Road, Southbourne, Bournemouth, Dorset, because it was a small all-girls independent school. It was located in my stepfather's hometown where he was born and brought up with his parents and seven brothers and sisters.

The SMG building was of a Victorian style, with white painted walls and black paint around the window frames and gutters. SMG was a Church Of England School for girls aged 5 to 18 years. The school was near the sea, about an altitude of 100 feet above sea level. The famous Shell House was only about five minutes' walk to Southbourne Over Cliffs. There were shell collections from all over the world; it was fascinating to look at, all the different colours and shapes of the shells were put together in an artistic form, which looked amazing and picturesque. I took many photos of the Shell House during the weekends when we were allowed out of the school compound in a group of three or more girls. There was another school house where the younger children boarded at night but walked about eight minutes to the main school compound. Mrs K M Cook was the owner and Principal of SMG. She was an elderly lady whom I admired, as she had so much zeal and enthusiasm in her spirit. She taught several subjects at school and she was very well spoken.

The beautiful shell house....

At St Mary's Gate School, 1982

Our routine each day at the boarding house was that we woke up about 06.30 a.m, queued for the bathroom, had a wash, then put on our uniforms, which was a maroon skirt with pleats, a matching jumper and blazer, a pink and white striped long sleeve shirt, for the winter, with a hat and a long beige winter coat. For the summer uniform, it was a pink and white striped dress, maroon cardigan, white gloves, and a straw hat with a maroon school logo at the front and also on the cape. The cape was strange for me, as I could not understand why it did not have sleeves, only holes to put your hands through. We also wore brown shoes with long white socks up to the knees. The winter PE uniforms were long maroon jogging bottoms, with the same matching long sleeved jogging sweater, with the school logo at the centre, with short white shoes. The summer PE uniform was a short maroon skirt with a white T-shirt and white sports shoes with white knee length socks. The uniforms were also sold at the school.

I was home-sick all the time, missing my old life in Sierra Leone. Now that I was locked away in a girls' boarding school, I felt all alone in this world. I used to look forward to my weekly phone calls from my parents in Saudi Arabia during the weekends. I never told them my real feelings, as I was afraid they would tell me off about how grateful I should be to attend a boarding school in England. This is the first time my parents will hear about the true feelings of my life in a boarding school in Bournemouth.

I struggled academically at school. Even though I enjoyed being at school and liked the routine, I was very empty inside. My smile was all people could see, so I wore it so well that it became part of my identity. Maths was my worst nightmare, I could hardly understand anything that was taught. I was willing to learn and always did all my homework, which was compulsory, anyway.

Our House Mistress was a strict lady but I liked her. I loved the way she used to pronounce my name "Ali...ma...tu". My first meal had Brussels sprouts, which I had never seen or eaten before. Because I refused to eat my vegetables I was sent upstairs with my dinner plate in my hand, into the Principal's office to explain myself. I knocked on the door of the Principal's office and I was told to enter. I stood there upright, as I was not afraid of anyone, and that included all adults. I explained the obvious reasons why I could not eat my sprouts, and I was told to try all the new food that was given to me, as this will help me to have a balanced diet. She showed some compassion. I walked down the stairs with the uneaten sprouts. I made that journey up those stairs a countless number of times, and then it finally stopped. It took me a very long time before I started enjoying the local food at school. I ended up liking most of my vegetables by the time I left St Mary's Gate School in 1987. Weekends were challenging for me as the girls got into their groups for going out after lunch. We had prep time to finish all our homework on Saturdays and Sundays. Then we were allowed to go out in groups for a few hours. No one seemed to want me in their clicks, a "typical girl thing". Our House Mistress noticed that this was a constant struggle for me, each weekend. She would suggest that I go out with a certain group of girls. I hated that because as soon as we left the school campus I would walk behind everyone else while they chatted with their best friends. I was mostly ignored throughout the trip, as we went by foot to Fisherman's Walk, Hengisbury Head or Southbourne Over Cliff. The only thing I used to look forward to was buying some Boom Booms from the sweet shop in Fisherman's Walk, which were my favourite sweets, as well as Bounty and Snickers. I loved the peanut as it reminded me of home, Sierra Leone. I thought about running away so many times, but I knew that the £1.50 pocket money couldn't take me back to Gatwick Airport, let alone buy me an air ticket to Freetown. I never discussed my plans with anyone; I did not get the chance to have a best friend. With everything I experienced in Moyamba with my father and step-mother, I didn't want to get attached to anyone emotionally so that I wouldn't get hurt or feel any pain. Even though I have always been an extrovert and love talking to people and getting to know them, I never got close to anyone. Something I had learnt at a very young age was never to have any attachments, that way you won't face disappointment.

When we woke up at SMG, we queued up for the bathroom, and after a quick wash we dressed in our uniforms and had to go downstairs for breakfast. Then school started at 08.30 a.m. and finished at 16:00 hours. We had a mid-morning break, and we were given cold milk with 2 biscuits. Lunchtime was either the main course with pudding, which was mostly sponge with custard, semolina, or vegetable soup with the main course.

My French teacher was kind to me, and even though I struggled with French, because she cared about me she didn't make a fuss. I made more effort to study French so that I could do well each week when we did our tests. She taught me the importance of learning 10-20 words each day in order to improve my French. Hence French became my favourite subject at school. I remember when I stayed with my French teacher and her family my first Christmas in England. I felt so welcomed in their home, loved and cared for by the whole family, including the students that were staying with her family. I also remember her quick wit and sense of humour when I dressed for the Fancy Dress Party as a baby wearing a large towel as a nappy, holding a teddy bear with a dummy in my mouth. My French teacher was like a mother to me; she was special and will remain in my heart forever. I was thankful to her for believing in me, it meant so much to me and I shall always treasure those memories. My second favourite class was literature, then history and then geography.

My other favourite yet interesting lesson which I attended on my own was elocution. My parents wanted me to speak posh The teacher was a middle-aged lady, and in our first lesson I had to look in a mirror in order to see how my lips moved when I spoke. Then she told me to repeat after her the following statements "O Martha had a castle near Derby rather smart". During this time the bottom of my jaw was supposed to drop, which was hilarious to watch in a mirror. Then I also had to repeat the next sentence "If the two too to Tooting was too soon to toot" my mouth was supposed to make an "O" shape with both my lips together. These lessons made me realise how difficult this language was. At least it was entertaining, and I had the lessons once a week. The teacher was very serious during these lessons; I had no idea how she kept a straight face while I was pronouncing those sentences. It's funny, when I was at school, almost all the teachers looked middle-aged. I would like to thank the few girls at SMG who made an effort to talk to me when you could and have kept in touch over the years. You know who you are, and I thank you for our continuous friendship. With me that meant a lot to me that and it still does.

I started at St Mary's Gate School in August 1982. My first night there was full of mixed emotions, as my mother and stepfather had to return to Saudi Arabia, where my stepfather was working for Aramco in Dhahran. Dhahran is a city located in the Eastern Province, it is a major administrative centre for the Saudi oil industry. Saudi Aramco Residential Camp in Dhadran was known by its inhabitants as the Dhahran Camp. This place was created solely for the staff at the Saudi Arabia Oil Company (Saudi Aramco). The compound had a fence around it and a security gate, with security guards checking who went in and out of the compound. It had its own airport, formerly known as Dhahran International Airport; it was the first airport ever built on Saudi Arabian soil and was opened by the United States Air Force from 1945 until 1962. It is now known as King Abudulaziz Air Base. Saudi Aramco, officially the Saudi Arabian Oil Company, so Saudi Arabian National Petroleum and Natural Gas Company is based in Dhahran. It is one of the largest companies in the world by revenue, and according to accounts by Bloomberg News, it is seen as the most profitable company in the world.

My mother and I used to use the Aramco bus to go shopping in Al-Khobar and Dammam. We would get dropped off to do some jewellery shopping then return back to Dhahran. My mother was a house-wife during that time.

My younger sister Jennifer and younger brother Andrew are my stepfather's children with my mother. They both attended Claysmore School, in Iwerne Minster, Blandford, Dorset, a co-educational day and boarding school for 2-18 year olds, from pre-prep and preschool. During our school holidays, Mr T would usually pick me up from St Mary's Gate School, and then we went to Claysmore to pick up my younger siblings, and then travel to Heathrow Airport to start our journey to Dhahran where our parents worked and lived. The air hostesses used to take care of us throughout our flight to Dhahran and we enjoyed all the fuss they made over us. They gave us activities to entertain ourselves during the flight, which was nice and thoughtful. When we arrived at Dhahran Airport, my stepfather would meet and pick us up with his car, which was a silver Chevrolet Impala, a spacious car with air-conditioning.

We would arrive at our house on Salamia Avenue, which had three bedrooms and a bathroom upstairs, while downstairs had the kitchen and a lounge area with a corridor. The air-conditioning was amazing, which made the house cooler, as the outside was usually hot. My step-father used to take the whole family to dinner in Dhahran, which was a nice treat, and the food was delicious. We also used to go to the cinema in Dhahran as well. I enjoyed spending our school holidays with our parents. I was happier while I was at home. These were precious family moments. My siblings and I travelled during our Christmas, Easter and summer school holidays. During the summer school holiday we would only spend two weeks in Dharan, and then return to Bournemouth where we would stay, but also travelled around England as a family.

Adulthood

When I left St Mary's Gate School, I applied to study in the Secretarial and Shorthand program at Bournemouth and Poole College. This was the beginning of my real adult life and I was not prepared for what I am about to tell you. I was no longer in boarding school where the adults made all the decisions about my life. Now I had to learn to adapt into a life in Bournemouth as a young lady. As I mentioned earlier, I worked for an agency that was based in The Triangle in Bournemouth, which meant I had the choice to work in different hotels, bars and casinos. This gave me lots of flexibility, as I could chose to work whenever and wherever. For the first time in my life, I could make decisions by myself. I was taking total control of my life and I was loving it. I was staying in my parents' house in Bournemouth while they were still living in Dhahran. There were many house rules but I managed to break nearly all of them. The house was situated in an affluent area of Talbot Woods in Bournemouth, and it had seven bedrooms. On the ground floor when you entered through the front door, on your left was a toilet, a sink, a toilet roll holder and a hook for a hand towel. Then there was another wooden door with four glass panels, same as the main front door. There was one step before you went into the main landing or corridor, and on the right was my bedroom, which had double bay windows. Almost opposite my bedroom was the staircase leading to the first floor, with the lounge door on the right at the bottom of the stairs. The lounge was large, 18ft by 16ft; it had high ceilings, just like the rest of the house. Opposite the lounge was another door with a small space for just hanging coats and storing shoes. Next to this door was another door leading off the corridor, and on the right side was a bathroom. Opposite that bathroom was the kitchen dining area, and to the left of that was the main kitchen. There was no door leading into the kitchen, just a doorframe. The kitchen had a gas hob. To the right was the gas oven, work-top, and then a window facing the back garden. The kitchen had a large Edwardian sink, two separate sinks; they were very deep with a kind of flat metal disc on the inside. The sink had a plug hole and plug in it. There was a switch to the right, which meant that it could have been used as a kind of washing machine during the period the house was built. On the right of the lounge was a large dining room, which was the same size as the lounge. The proportions of these old houses were designed during the late Edwardian period, giving an impressive amount of spaciousness. The high ceilings allowed the flow of hot air to induce cool air from the windows to be circulated within the space in the summer.

Just below the ceilings were dados around each room, which are used for hanging pictures. On the left side of the kitchen were wall units, more than half of that wall was an arch-way made of glass, with two large glass panels, which could be opened by sliding the glass panels to the left or right. This arch-way was used to pass food through to the dining room on special occasions when we had guests visiting our family. The kitchen also had a large dining table that could seat six people, while the main dining room had a large thick oak table, with chunky legs, that could seat from eight to ten people. There were massive bay windows which overlooked the back garden, which was roughly the size of a tennis court. A garage was at the end of the garden also with a drive-way. The house had three side gates, including the garage gates. At the front of the house, when you walked through the main gate, the path was all concrete, with lawns on either side.

The first floor had five bedrooms, and at the top of the stairs was a very spacious landing. On the right was a guest room with fitted wardrobes, and next to that was another door that led to my sister Jenny's bedroom by a narrow flight of stairs. When you got to the top, the attic door was on the right, and the whole attic was the length and width of the entire house from that outer wall. Opposite the attic was Jenny's bedroom; the bedroom had a window overlooking the back garden of the house. Her bed was on the left side of the room, which had a slope at the head of her bed and a sink on the right side of her bed with a towel holder. The attic room was a very spacious square room, with a built-in fitted wardrobe. Next to the attic's main door was a hallway that turned right. It had a door, which was like a small store room, and then the main family bathroom.

As you entered the bathroom, the toilet was in front of you, and the wall between the toilet and the bath tub was black with an arch. All the walls were tiled in black, and the hand wash basin was on the right side hand side of the bath, followed by a large mirror opposite the bath, with a round ceiling light. To the right of the bathroom was another double bedroom, and the windows overlooked the back garden of the house. That was my main bedroom, which I only used when the whole family was together during the holidays. It was easier for me to use the guest room downstairs when I was living alone in the house. Coming towards the main landing was the smallest bedroom in the house which my step-father used as his office. He displayed all his collections of books that he had gathered all those years he lived in Sierra Leone and other parts of Africa. He also displayed his university degrees, which he studied for in Dharan, Saudi Arabia, via Indian University of North America through correspondence, which was funded by Aramco, the oil company my step-father worked for at that time. He was so proud of all his framed certificates displayed on all the wall space in that room. Nobody in the family was allowed to go sit in the room, except for when he wanted to discuss all the qualifications of each framed certificate. He used to sit in his study listening to his classical music, which he loves. There was a very large mirror between his office and Andrew's bedroom Next to my stepfather's office was my younger brother Andrew's bedroom, which was a massive bedroom with a bay window facing the back garden. Next to Andrew's bedroom was my parents' bedroom, which also had a large bay window facing the front of the house. There were large fitted wardrobes on the left side as you entered the bedroom, two small windows opposite the wardrobes, and a 6ft bed between the small windows. The bed was an unusual shape; it was shaped like a heart. This bed was bought with the property in the mid-1980s. My stepfather worked for Aramco from 1975-1992, and Aramco paid 75% of our school fees, including our boarding school fees. I am so grateful to have had that privilege, even though as a young teenager I did not appreciate it at that time. As I got older I realised how blessed I was to be that kid from the east end of Freetown Sierra Leone and attending a boarding school in England. During those days it was such a massive blessing indeed and I thank God for His goodness throughout my life.

After I left school in 1987, I got a part-time job "Modelling" as I had a 24 inches waist line with a 34D Chest, and 38 inches-hips and 5ft 6" tall, I was hoping for a career as a model, but the Agent wanted me to take all my clothes off, which I refused to do, hence that job only lasted for few weeks.

These are the photos from my modelling days.

When I finished school I had no idea about living independently on my own so I lived with my parents in their house. I loved having a large house to myself. I broke all the house rules by having parties every month, inviting over fifty friends on a Saturday night, and partying till dawn. I hope when my parents read this book that I have written, they will not be shocked. I loved going to the gym on my own or with friends, as you do when you are at that age. The gym I went to was for ladies only. It was situated near the Lansdowne area, which was close to Bournemouth College, which I attended during that period. The gym had a ground floor where all the machines were, including the shower rooms.

Then on the first floor was the dance studio, which was used for dance classes. I had loved dancing and singing since I was a very young child. My typical routine would be to wake up at 07.00 a.m., wash and get dressed, and eat breakfast. My favourite cereals were Corn Flakes and Rice Crispies. Then I walked up the road to get a bus to Lansdowne. As I stood at the bus stop, after seeing a bus in the distance, I would put my hand out to stop the bus, but the bus would not stop for me for some unknown reason. Then I would decide to walk to the gym. After the gym and dance class, I would again walk to the nearest bus stop by the gym, but this time because there were other people at the bus stop the driver would stop and allow me to get on. This pattern continued for many years. Then one day during college break I was asking the other students if they had experienced the bus drivers ignoring them at bus stops. Then, the penny dropped. All those years I was at boarding school, I never experienced racism from any of the girls. Most of the issues at school were the normal girl issues, the usual clicks, the best friend labels and so on. I did not have any best friends at school, which never bothered me as I was already used to that throughout my childhood. Being an extrovert, nobody would have dared to bully me at that time. I was always polite, kind, and caring, and could make conversations easily with people who also wanted to make conversation with me. I loved my own company, and also used to spend a lot of my time reading Mills & Boon, which were popular romantic fiction books. I found reading therapeutic and I loved the different places I could go while reading.

My classmates at college were shocked about the bus stop issue. It never occurred to me that, even though there were a handful of black people living in Bournemouth in 1985, racism was an issue. I had probably experienced racism while I was at school without realising it. I knew certain girls did not like me for some unknown reason, especially the heads of the clicks. My main purpose at school was to learn, and I focused on that mainly. Anything else would have been a bonus. I have always been a confident lady with an outgoing personality, and I wear my smile very well, which had become part of my DNA. I was lucky to have had that firm foundation from my grandmother who brought me up. I have always lived my whole life in gratitude and appreciate all the little things in life. I have a happy and content life, and I am also very grateful for everything in my life.

The bus stop issues continued. I tried to report it to a bus conductor. He just ignored me, and might have been more racist than the bus driver that refused to stop his bus for me.

One afternoon I was walking home from college, when two men in their car shouted the "N" word at me, plus their two fingers as well. Their car was driving towards at that time. I carried on walking; I could not believe that this was really happening to me. I got home, cried a lot and could not eat anything for the rest of the day. I decided to cancel my evening out with the group of girls I attended the gym with.

The next morning it was raining. Again I walked to the bus stop, my hand out, but no luck again. This became a way of life for me in Bournemouth. If I did get lucky to be on a bus, no one would ever sit next to me, another normal daily occurrence. I started experiencing racism every week: name-calling, eggs and pens thrown at me by people in their cars. I stopped talking about the issue with the people I knew. I told my parents about what was happening to me. Up to the present day in Bournemouth, I still get called names at least once a month. It's sad that people can just judge you by the colour of your skin. I have not experienced any racism in other parts of England, and I have travelled across almost the entire country, with the exception of few places.

I learnt to dislike the question people always ask when they meet you "Where are you from?" I stopped answering that question. People should be able to do small talk without bringing up racial topics in a conversation. I used to love going out on Saturday and Sunday afternoons for roller-skating with disco at Glen Fern Road. It was fun meeting new people and enjoying dancing as well. Some of the nightclubs that were popular at that time were The Venue, and Tower Park in Poole was a massive nightclub which opened in the late 1980s. Saturday evenings were amazing, as I shared taxi with friends to take us there. The nightclub had few large stages that played different music. It closed in 1999. Some other popular locations were Zoo & Cage, The Elements, Berlin, Spat, and Opera House in Boscombe. Jumping Jack IMAX opened in 1999 as part of the waterfront complex, near Bournemouth Pier. There was also Bumbles at the Triangle, Alcatraz at the Lansdowne, Madison in the Square where I celebrated my 21st birthday, and Zig Zags. People travelled from different parts of the country for the fun nightlife in Bournemouth.

My Parents and siblings

"You Are Never Too Old To Set Another Goal Or To Dream A New Dream."

~C.S. Lewis

CHAPTER 5
THE DIVORCE

Fear of divorce can be paralyzing. You know that it is probably the right thing to do, but you feel extremely dumb for not being able to put it all together. The ending of a relationship is in no way flowers and sunshine like the beginning of it is. When you end a relationship, a bunch of emotions come to a sudden halt and make you feel numb. The situation is undefinable, which portrays how hard it is.

Why is divorce scary? The majority of people fear divorce, and according to statistics, women fear it the most. The biggest dilemma with women is that they are scared of being a single parent. It is not because they don't possess the strength that pulls them together, or because they feel incomplete without their significant other. The main issue is the struggle to deal with the heartbreak and also manage your duty as a parent perfectly. Men usually drop out of the marriage, leaving the child with the mother. The situation thus doubles up on the woman who has to fight her emotions and deal with her child.

Moreover, the mindset of not being able to provide an entire world of happiness to their child, without their father, seems devastating for the woman. Society plays a huge role in this as people judge a single parent and how the "poor" child is missing out on the love of the other parent. Thus, the biggest fear during divorce is not just the breakup of two people; it has to do a lot with what the entire family has to go through.

On the 11th of September 2001, I moved out of my marital home with my two children. A few months later, I was told by my solicitor that I should return to my marital home, which I did in November 2001. My children and I stayed there till enough was enough and we moved out.

The divorce left me as a single parent raising both my children. I was filled with so many mixed emotions. However, I had to pull myself together to be able to look after them and ensure they didn't feel disturbed about the whole situation. I wanted them to feel loved and cared for.

In 2002, when I moved into the flat where I am still living, my GP had signed me off with stress during these challenging times. I did not know where to turn and what to do, as my journey of being a single parent had started. I noticed that when I tried to contact my married friends I knew before, they were not showing any interest in our friendship any more. There was a sense of rejection, being ignored. They had lots of excuses not to chat with me on the phone or to meet up. They stopped coming to my home with their children. Conversations happened less and less and less. It took me many months to realise that the only reason these people were friends with me was because I was a married woman with children.

That was my first wakeup call as a single parent. Being off sick meant I could grieve over my new challenges, and adjust to my new ways of life with my two year old toddler, my daughter, and my four year old son.

River of Emotions

Ending a union is tough, especially when you are in a bond that is meant to last forever. Marriage is not just about love, but is a combination of understanding, compromises and decisions. Thus, when it ends, a river of emotions overflows. You feel angry at yourself and your partner for not being able to get everything together. You blame yourself over and over for not giving it a chance. Sudden rage and anger ends with a pool of tears that is hard to overcome or control.

The emotional rollercoaster starts with denial as you find it difficult to believe that the thing you feared the most is happening to you. Denial is very common during divorce, especially for partners who have spent a lot of good time together. This is commonly followed by anxiety and panic attacks where you feel lost and usually fall into depression. The emotional rollercoaster only ends with acceptance and letting go of what is done and dusted. It does take some time, but you eventually do get there.

Tips for Dealing with Divorce and Depression

Dealing with divorce can be devastating, and there is only one way out of it: acceptance! You need to accept that a beautiful relationship has come to an end and it won't be with you along the journey. According to experts, here are some things that one can practice to deal with depression:

People tend to indulge in negative self-talk after divorce. You must talk positively and be very careful about what you tell yourself. Think and talk positive, and you will notice a greater change.

Interact with people around you. The biggest issue with divorced people is that they isolate themselves because they don't want to answer a lot of questions that people might ask them. It is best to be open and talk about it or indulge in a fun conversation with friends or hang out to enjoy the other side of life.

Before I went back to work full-time, I was lucky to find a childminder who was living next to the school, my children were attending. I am so grateful to have found this kind and caring lady. My kids were happy with her, she always did activities with them, which they brought home. After all the experiences I had received from people I had known for many years who no longer wanted me in their lives because I was a single mother, I soon got used to being alone. This was something I had experienced as a very young child growing up in Sierra Leone.

My children were attending junior primary school. My new childminder normally looked after children from about 8 a.m. in the morning, but she was willing to look after my two children when we met for the first time and I told her that I needed to be at work for 7 a.m. I felt really blessed to have her. My childminder was empathetic towards my children and I felt grateful to her.

After grieving for several months, after the separation I decided I had to bounce back; my children needed me. I had neglected, isolated and rejected myself. I started wearing only jogging bottoms, even though I wasn't a trousers person. This was all part of my grieving process. I tried to bounce back, remembering my grandmother's wise words that this was all part of life's experiences and I would have to learn from them and concentrate on the children. I had to count myself lucky, because having children from my marriage kept me focused on them and I assured myself that I was young enough to meet someone in the future. Every time you fall into the trap of depression and worthlessness, always remember the word gratitude. Try to think of all the things you have to be grateful for in your life and repeat that in your mind.

I was a full-time working mother. After my maternity leave had finished I returned back to work immediately. I loved being a working mother, even though it was very hard to balance two young children who were in full-time school plus being a mother with a full-time job. I kept going, focusing mainly on my children's wellbeing. I was involved in every aspect of my children's lives, taking them to the park to play on the swings, running around the common with a football, doing Rounders, Cricket, playing card games at home as well as Ludo, Snakes and Ladders, and even Monopoly, during which my son would always buy all the posh properties. My son was very smart and appeared to understand the value of money even within the board game of Monopoly. My daughter was always lucky with the Ludo games, she always won. As for me, Snakes and Ladders was my worst nightmare, because as soon as I got to the top of the ladder, I would roll my dice and the number that would come up would send me to the tail of the snake. I could not understand why that kept on happening, but it was all part of not taking life too seriously. My children appeared content and happy. Communication was very important, and the number one skill that was taught at home was table manners and to respect one another. I taught my children to be transparent, honest, kind, to remember to wash their hands and tidy up when they made a mess, especially with toys and books.

I managed to arrange to work Monday to Friday, and then have the weekends off. I always booked annual leave around my children's half term and school holidays. Money was tight, but we made it happen.

When I got paid at the end of each month, my mortgage was the most important bill to be paid, followed by all the utility bills, including council tax, water, sewage, gas, electricity, building insurance, telephone, and mobile bills. Then I bought my monthly bus pass for work, as I don't drive. With whatever was left, I would buy our food, including pack lunches for the children to take to school. We had hardly any money left after everything was paid for. I would then have to use my credit cards to survive with my children. Being in debt was just a way of life, buying two sets of school uniforms was expensive every summer, especially for my son as he used to wear out his trousers in the knees and jumpers in the elbows very quickly, as he loved crawling on the floor. He could hardly sit in one place for more than a few minutes, always on the move, a very active child.

Saffi, my daughter, was a text book baby. She was out of her nappy around 18 months old; fascinated with the toilet seat, she did not like the idea of sitting on a potty. She just wanted to sit on a proper toilet. I eventually bought her a stool that she could put her feet on. Then, she loved her foot stool and felt so grown up. Whereas my son, Amza, was over two years old before he was out of his nappy. As soon as his younger sister was born, when I arrived home with my baby daughter, he was excited for the first few weeks. Then he wanted more attention from me. He thought his sister was taking up too much of my time. My son hardly slept during the day and was also a poor night sleeper; he had chronic eczema, which made him itch. I tried so many ointments, different creams the dermatologists prescribed to help relieve his discomfort, but none of that worked. By the time he started full time school he was four years old, and the eczema was stable but still itchy. The night times were very difficult for Amza, but he managed to get some sleep. Amza has loved reading and drawing cartoons since he was about two years old when he was watching Sonic. He began to draw, read and also started writing. I encouraged him to develop these skills, as he concentrated 100% on whenever he was drawing and reading. I noticed he appeared to have a gift and helped him develop his drawing skills. At the age of about eight, Amza started doing stories with cartoon characters.

At the start of the week, on Monday mornings, I would normally wake up at 05.00 a.m., and get washed and dressed. The packed lunches for the kids would have been done the night before. I would wake Saffi up, help her to wash and get ready for school, then wake Amza up, and also assisted him with getting ready. We would all eat breakfast together at about 05.50 am, and then leave our flat just after 06.05am. We would walk to the childminder's house, which was a ten minute walk. As soon as my childminder opened her front door I would rush to catch my bus at 06.35 am.

I would arrive at work just on time before handover. I worked for a local NHS hospital caring for people living with dementia. I cared for both male and female clients. Even though the job was challenging, it was also rewarding to be able to care, support and look after some of the most vulnerable people in our society.

The Effects of Divorce on Children

If you have children who are sensitive or are above 1 and a half years old, then it is not only you who is going through the divorce. It is not only you who needs to bounce back to life; you need to take significant steps to help them too. The first year is the toughest to deal with as you are setting boundaries, and you don't know whether you will make it through or not. Also, there is so much to decide, like whether you should allow the other parent to see the child or not.

There is a lot that goes through a child's mind during the divorce process:

An emotional mess is the biggest effect of divorce on kids. They fail to understand why they have to go from one home to the other. They struggle to understand the situation and get used to it. The largest confusion caused here is that these children don't believe in love as they have seen and experienced it end in front of their eyes. Thus, they turn out to be a little emotionally numb.

Teenagers usually turn into angry monsters and do not accept the situation. The best way to deal is to sit with them and communicate the issue and make them understand that it is a mutual decision, and they need to accept it.

Children find it very hard to accept their parents' divorce, but once it's done, it is best to help them deal with it as you are helping yourself.

Divorce is a huge decision to make, but it is best to part ways from anyone who doesn't seem good for you or your life. Sometimes it is good for both partners. Thus, if you have taken a step, it is best to stick to it and fight the circumstances with all your strength. Bounce back to life and help your kids get back to life as well.

During my separation stage. I went through crazy phases but my smile never changed.....

"Things Work Out Best For
Those Who Make The Best Of
How Things Work Out."

~ John Wooden

CHAPTER 6
LIFE AS A SINGLE PARENT

Being a single parent is stressful; it is not all sunshine, but it is not entirely gloomy days and rainy mornings either. Raising a child on your own, without the emotional support of a loving partner, can make things tough, but there are a few things that can help you manage well.

Use your words to show love:

Many single parents are so stressed that they forget to put their love into words. Remember that your child is equally upset in this situation and is missing out on the love of their father or mother. Thus, make sure that you say what you want to and let them know that you love them. Being expressive and showing your love will help them be more confident. Your support and unconditional love will make them powerful and important.

No guilt should be involved:

Make sure that you do not spoil your child due to the guilt of being a single parent. If you are trying to make up for the other parent, then don't. This will not only ruin you emotionally but will also spoil the kid, which will not be good for you in the long run. You need to be straightforward about your expectations with your child without being guilty. You both are in this together.

Set some limitations:

Finances can be chaotic for a single parent. It is just you earning and running the house. Until and unless you have a lot of money, it is best to set some limits financially. Every month, discuss your budget with your child and involve them in making a list of all the household priorities. Once that is done, if you have any space left in the budget, you can ask your child for what they want. Or you can keep one thing per week which excites them. Set friendly limitations; thus, the child does not feel bad. Also, involving them in making grocery lists will help you in raising a responsible child who understands your position, too.

Don't forget yourself:

As a single parent, one usually forgets themselves. However, you must not do this. Make sure that you take care of yourself both mentally and physically. Get a good 7-8 hours of sleep and make sure that you eat healthy, too. Remember that if you don't take care of yourself, how will you take care of your child? Stay healthy!

Stay positive:

It is certainly easier said than done, but one can always try. Stay positive as much as you can. What is done is done, and your partner won't come back to you. Thus, always look on the brighter side and teach your child the same thing. Tell him or her that things will get better and teach them that life is still beautiful, no matter what the given situation might be. This will help you raise a positive and happy child.

Separation or divorce is very stressful for the parents, but it is very depressing for the child too. If your child is a teenager, you will find the circumstances to be more difficult to deal with. However, with some little tips and effort, you can create a happy and friendly environment for your kids and yourself. Just hang in there, and things will turn out to be just fine.

My children and I......

If a child lives with criticism, he learns to blame.
If a child lives with aggression, she learns to fight.
If a child is made fun of, he learns to be shy.
If a child lives in fear, she learns to be timid.
If a child lives in shame, he learns to feel guilty.

BUT...

If a child lives with tolerance, she learns to be
patient.
If a child lives with encouragement, he learns to be
confident.

If a child lives with praise, she learns to appreciate.
If a child lives with fairness, he learns justice.
If a child lives with security, she learns to trust.
If a child and his belongings receive respect, he will
respect and value others.
If a child lives with approval, she learns to like
herself.
If a child lives with acceptance and friendship, he
learns to find love in the world.

~ Dorothy Law-Nolte

CHAPTER 7
AUTISM

Autism is quite a complex neurobehavioural situation that includes issues with social interactions and communication. It is a developmental disability that has no permanent solution and is lifelong. People struggling with autism, have a completely different world, and their communication skills are opposite to what they are for normal people. There is a huge range of symptoms of autism, and that is why this medical disorder is now termed as Autism Spectrum disorder. It also varies in severity; some might have a very complicated autism situation while some might not be very critical.

Life for people with autism is hard as they have difficulty understanding what other people are telling them, and likewise, they find it challenging to communicate their needs to others as well. It is not just about communicating verbally; they also find it hard to express something through expressions as well, and they are usually not touch friendly, too. The communication impairment makes it a struggle for autism patients to live a very normal life, but with several medical advancements, we are now experiencing a huge change in the situation.

Symptoms of Autism:

The symptoms of autism are usually quite visible in the first three years of a child. You will be able to notice communication and developmental impairments within a year or two of your child's birth. This dilemma is usually more common in boys than in girls.

The first thing that one can notice in a child with autism is that they don't make eye contact. Lack of good, normal eye contact is the very first sign. The child might focus on one item a lot or for an abnormally extended time. If your child is above 2 or 3 and they do not interact socially with other kids, than this can be a sign too. The symptoms of autism vary, but make sure that your child is not interacting with you or others in an abnormal way before you get finicky. A slight lack of interaction is not autism, but if it is lingering a lot, then it is best to visit a doctor.

Characteristics of Autism:

Here is a list of traits of autism that can help you pinpoint it:

• Social interaction problems

Not understanding the body language of another person is a huge characteristic of autism. Also, being unable to understand how to interact in a social environment along with having difficulty in maintaining or developing relationships with people are traits of autism.

• Behavioural Pattern Issues

People with autism get highly upset with slight environmental changes and behave aggressively or weird. They have a very narrow group of interests and don't try to step out of them. Repetitive behaviour is also a huge trait of autism. Repeating one thing over and over again without realizing is a sign that the person might have autism.

Parenting a Child with Autism:

Having a child with autism is stressful because you are worried about their future and how they will deal with environmental changes as they grow up. This is normal because you have to find a way to help them.

Firstly, don't try to enforce the situation on them. Keep steering them in a positive direction. It is not going to be easy but keep trying. Every child responds to affirmation, and it is best that you start it from the moment your child gets diagnosed with it.

Children with autism are very finicky about routine. Thus, it is best that you create very positive surroundings for them and make a proper schedule which involves interaction and constant communication. Try to make them learn new skills so that they are constantly stepping outside their comfort zone. Never make a child with autism very comfortable with just one thing. Explore with them so that they are always eager to learn more.

Involve your child in activities. This is going to be exhausting to do daily, but it is best to do it on a routine basis. This will keep your child interacting, and that is what you need to focus on. You need to treat your child through a professional too, but along with treatment, you need to do everything possible to make sure that your child does not have to face a lot of problems in the future with communicating with people around them.

My son had Asperger's syndrome (AS), also known as Asperger's, which is under the umbrella of autism and is a developmental disorder characterised by significant difficulties in social interaction and nonverbal communication, along with restricted and repetitive patterns of behaviour and interests as defined by science. Despite having good language skills, people with AS may sound over-precise or over-literal. Jokes can cause problems as can exaggerated language, turns of phrase and metaphors.

My son was first diagnosed with special needs in 2003, when his teacher in Year 2 noticed that he appeared to have increased rocking movements, thumb sucking and random arm movements. He was not sure what to do with himself. He would crawl around the floor and would find it difficult to start tasks without support. Amza tended to invade other children's space; he was not aware of the effects of his behaviour on the other pupils, he rarely showed emotions facially and appeared not to recognise it in other people.

He took a great interest in posters and factual information posters posted on the wall and became overly engrossed in some activities. He particularly liked to make and keep Lego models in the same place in the classroom. He had a favourite chair and became upset if anyone else used it. He continues to read, which he has enjoyed from a very young age

The primary school that he was attending agreed to take action to help Amza. The school implemented strategies appropriate for pupils with social and communication difficulties. Some of these were discussed, including the use of visual cues, giving clear beginnings and endings to tasks, and ensuring Amza's name was used before a direct request or instruction. The use of the word "stop" when his activities were annoying others was introduced, both to him and for others to use. This helped, and consideration was given to providing other short instructions which were arranged by a visual cue where necessary. The school introduced a visual timetable using photographs of Amza doing the activities, so that he could gain a clear routine and know when new tasks/activities began and ended. The idea of using a carpet square for Amza during the whole class carpet time was tried, so that he was clear about where he should be. He seems to work better when at a table with other students, so although the idea of a "work station" was discussed it felt not to be as helpful. However, in view of his anxieties, he may be helped by knowing his favourite table so that it can be reserved for him, or at least knowing which table he should sit at for which activities.

As a mother, I found it helpful when I asked the school if I could be present in his class so that I could see my son's activity and then compare it with his behaviour at home and share ideas with the school. He was referred to a speech and language assessment

As soon as we meet a person we make judgements about them; just by looking we can often guess their status, and by the expression on their face or the tone of their voice, we can usually tell whether they are happy, angry or sad and respond accordingly. Not everyone has the natural ability. People with Asperger Syndrome find it more difficult to read the signal which of us take for granted. As a result they find it more difficult to communicate and interact with others,

Asperger's syndrome is a form of autism, a condition that affects the way a person communicates and relates to others. A number of the traits of autism are common to Asperger's syndrome. However, people with Asperger's syndrome usually have fewer problems with language than those with autism, often speaking fluently, though these words can sometimes sound formal or stilled. People with AS do not have the accompanying learning disabilities associated with autism. In fact, people with AS are often of average or above average intelligence. Because of this, many children with AS enter mainstream schools and with the right support and encouragement, can make good progress an go on to further education and employment. People with AS like to socialise and enjoy human contact. They do find it hard to understand non-verbal signals, including facial expressions, which makes it more difficult for them to form and make a relationship with people unaware of their needs. People with AS may speak fluently but they may not take notice of the reaction of the people listening to them, and they may talk on and on regardless of the listeners' interest or they may appear insensitive to their feelings. They might be confused or frightened by a statement like "she bit my head off". In order to help a person with AS to understand you, keep your sentences short - be clear and concise.

People with AS often develop an almost obsessive interest in a hobby or collecting. My son has been drawing Sonic since he was about 2 years and 6 months old, which he enjoys, and has become a permanent hobby for him. I was lucky as a single parent that my son had an early diagnosis, and most of all he has had the necessary support and understanding to be able to attend mainstream school and secondary school where a training session was given for AS Level before he started. Of course, there are sometimes problems but he is just treated as a "difficult" child, which could easily be the case if his condition were not understood.

When Amza was younger, his diet was limited to only few items of food, which were plain white bread with butter, tuna pasta, spaghetti Bolognese, roast chicken, roast potatoes and chips with burgers. I am very grateful to The National Autistic Society which funded and brought training workshops to Bournemouth during those early years, which has helped me as a mother to support my son. I also want to thank the NHS Trust that I have worked for all these years, which allowed me to take the time to attend all those training sessions. I have learnt a lot from the workshop training, implementing everything that was taught, which has given my son this opportunity to be able to leave home and go to university. He is still doing his drawing, but this time he is studying Animation and Illustration at university. He also had the opportunity to go to California last year in August 2018, through a student exchange to attend California State University of Long Beach (CalState).

Even though Amza has lots of challenges at university, he keeps in touch with me constantly, sending WhatsApp messages every day, and also chatting about his feelings, about university, the courses he is studying, making new friends, trips to LA, Warner Brother's Studios, Disney. He had an incredible time in California and I am very proud of him. I thank God for all His grace and mercy.

Dealing with a child who has autism is challenging, but it is not impossible. Go to a professional and get your child treated for it. The earlier, the better! Also, don't give up on them and keep trying. You can push them through their bubble and develop their communication skills. The real treatment starts from home, and you as a parent can deal with them much better as they are close to you.

I will never forget that faithful afternoon when my son's paediatrician gave me the news that the diagnosis was definite. The first question I asked her was "if he would ever leave home?" Her reply was "it depends on what kind of mother you become to this little boy" then she named a few very famous people in the world who were living with this condition and still have a fulfilling life. I knew from that moment onwards my life as a single mother was going to be different to say the least. I was going to be learning lots of new skills for my son.

"Develop An 'Attitude Of Gratitude'. Say Thank You To Everyone You Meet For Everything They Do For You."

~ Brian Tracy

CHAPTER 8
COMPLEX PELVIC ABDOMINAL PAIN FOLLOWING SURGERY

Up to summer of 2017, I was a fit and healthy woman. My neighbour had just become a new personal trainer and was willing to support me with a keep-fit programme. I started to do jogging, boxing, and other exercise, which I was enjoying. Before that, I was attending my weekly dance classes, which were salsa and belly dancing, which have been my hobbies throughout my life. I love what dancing does to me, it sends me to another place where I get lost with a very happy feeling. A natural high! I enjoy playing tennis, mostly in the Summer months. Gym was my second home, as I worked very hard to maintain my 24 inch waist line, which I was so proud of!

I found out at the beginning of May 2017 that there was going to be a Twilight Walk for Women's Health, which was to raise money for the Women's Health Unit at the Royal Bournemouth Hospital. I was excited to tell my daughter and personal trainer about the news; both ladies were happy to join the good cause to give me some support. I was very happy with their responses, so I trained really hard so that I could achieve those goals. I registered with the hospital charity, got my pink T-shirt and I went and bought myself matching pink jogging bottoms, with a hoody to match my T-shirt. When I got home, couldn't wait to show my daughter. I was doing extra training the days I didn't see my personal trainer. I would jog to the park, round the field and back home. I was enjoying it so much that I kept working out almost seven days a week. I told my work colleagues about the great cause and they were happy to sponsor me. Out of 72 staff, more than 75% supported me, and I was grateful for their kindness. In total, my sponsorship money was just under £200, which I gave to the hospital charity.

On the 19th of May 2017, the date of the charity walk, the weather was glorious. At 07.45 pm, you wouldn't have known it was that time in the evening, the sun was glowing in the clear blue sky, and there were hundreds of women who had come down to support our local hospital. We all did a 15 minutes warm-up exercise, and then the real walk started at 08.00 pm. I suddenly hurried to get past as many people as I could because of the large crowd. I was on a mission to achieve my 5 kilometres in less than an hour. I was extremely pleased to achieve the 5 kilometres in 46 minutes. I just found this strength from somewhere, and I surprised myself. My daughter and my personal trainer could not believe what they were seeing. Then from a distance, I could see the end of the line, that last hundred meters. I started to run, until I arrived at the finish line. That was a joyous moment for me. This was the first time in my life to have done a charity contribution that was personal to me, even though I have supported and sponsored hundreds of people in my lifetime at different stages in my life.

I carried on with my training, keeping fit and healthy, and eating fresh cooked meals that I enjoy making at home for my family and I. I played tennis in the summer months, and even managed to get a few of my colleagues to join me after work. It was fun, but I loved the fact that I was always a strong component, as the saying goes "Never judge a book by its cover".

The day for my surgery arrived, my children and my partner escorted me that Tuesday morning. When we arrived in the waiting room, I registered with the man who was seated behind the reception desk. He told me to wait for the nurse to call me in. I sat down for few minutes, then went into the corridor. I was beginning to feel nervous about the surgery. The nurse called out my name, I gave my family hugs and kisses, as I went off to prepare for my surgery. I told my family that they would need to call the hospital before they visit me on the Ward that evening. They left and I waved good bye to them and blew some kisses.

The nurse directed me into a side room where I was supposed to change into a hospital gown, which was beige with white stripes. The hospital was painted beige with a grey coloured square patterns. I had to sign all the usual legal documents before surgery. Then it was my turn to go into the operating theatre. I never knew I had so many nerves in my body until that moment in time. As I lay on the theatre bed, there were about five staff in the room. They asked my name and started small talk to distract me from my nerves, but I knew too well what their intentions were. Then the last thing I remembered was that I was supposed to count to 15, so I started counting: 1, 2, 3, 4, 5... I'm not sure what happened after that. I don't have any recollection of when I was taken into the recovery room, heavily sedated. I could hear lots of people talking, and the nurse who was looking after me kept calling my name. I wasn't sure if I was dreaming. I managed to open my eyes; the lights were bright and I felt discomfort with the lights on, even though I was not 100% awake. When I finally woke up properly, I was told that I was the only patient left in the recovery room. By then it was 8pm and time for the nurse to finish her duty. The nurse was kind, and she took me into the ward where I was going to recover after my surgery and told me that the surgery went well. I was so happy to see my children and partner. They stayed for a short while, as I was very drowsy. The night staff nurse had arrived, and she came and introduced herself to me, and gave me some medication. I could barely move, as I was very sore from having open surgery. I spent five days in hospital. My children came to visit me twice a day. I was poorly but wanted to go home to be with my children. My Consultant arrived each morning with his team of medical staff to ask how I was doing, they were nice, compassionate and explained details of my scan results. I lost all my sensation due to the surgery, but I was told everything would go back to normal soon. Lots of people that knew I was in hospital came to visit me, brought get well cards, fruits, chocolates, and all sorts of different types of gifts. I had no appetite for food or drinks.

After I arrived home that Saturday evening, I was still in a lot of pain but I was happy to be home. My children and my partner looked after me well; I had hardly eaten in the hospital. My friends made me a light soup. Others bought me ready-made soups. My kitchen looked like a Floret shop. My church family also came to visit me at the hospital and at home. I was grateful for all the people that were praying for me across the world. My daughter encouraged me to have some soup, and I managed to sip a small amount. I went to sleep that night. When I woke on Sunday, I felt more ill than while I was in hospital. I carried on taking all my medication and my injections to prevent a blood clot.

Went to bed that evening, woke up to use the toilet, and then I knew something was seriously wrong. My daughter called 111, and explained to the lady on the other end of the phone that her mum was very ill. All her observations were abnormal, but because I was still breathing normally, she did not think I needed an ambulance. Then my daughter called again, and explained to another operator that she decided to send an emergency doctor over. When they arrived at my house, they came into the bedroom where I was lying, looked at me and decided to call an ambulance straight away. I was readmitted into hospital. When I arrived there I was taken to have a scan. When I had the scan, it showed that I had an infection. My consultant was very kind as he waited outside Radiology Department to meet me and showed empathy towards me. I was taken to my ward by the hospital porter.

I spent another nine days in hospital again, still in so much pain. Then there were other complications after the infection. From the first day I had the infection, I was in pain every blessed day, 24 hours a day. I was told that things would settle eventually. On the second day back in the hospital, the night staff had their handover. A female nurse came into my ward, which was a six-bedded room. My bed was on the right, and there were three beds on each side of the room. My bed was the second on the right. They walked in, greeted the patient to my left, the ones opposite me, then the patient to my right, and then ignored me, literally. I could not believe what was going on. So during medication, when this same nurse came to give me medication, I refused, as I could not trust her. I thought to myself, so racism does exist in hospitals as well. I did not make any complaint or tell anyone at the hospital. I only told my family, and told them not to make any fuss about my bad experience with that nurse. Fortunately for me I was moved to another ward the following day. I wondered up to now how many other people had experienced racism in hospitals across England.

I was discharged home, and my pain continued. Follow-up appointments were given to me. I was in and out of hospital so regularly that it became a way of life for me and my children. Christmas came and went, and the New Year. I was told that things would settle, and I waited and waited. Easter came and went, and then in spring of 2018 my consultant decided that he would do a key-hole surgery to see exactly what was going on since my last surgery in the summer of 2017. My abdominal pain carried on. I had a diagnostic laparoscopy. I was told that there were risks with this procedure on the day I was admitted again into hospital. During the laparoscopy, it was found that I needed to have another further procedure; there were major injuries, which had left me worse off than before. But I am grateful to be alive after all the procedures I have had done, and I thank God, my Almighty Father, for His grace and mercy in my life. I was told before the procedure was done that there were risks involved. After 22 months, I am learning to live with this chronic pain, even though I have been through so much since I had my first surgery in the summer of 2017. I have manged to do another charity walk for my local hospital this June 2019. I walked 5 kilometres in 44 minutes, which meant I beat my previous record in May 2017 by two minutes. My family was so proud of me. I am blessed to have family and friends that care about me, and my church family who are always praying for me.

Living with chronic pain can be extremely exhausting, both mentally and physically. Accepting that intense pain is a part of your life can be devastating. But that is certainly not the end of life. If you look at the brighter side, there is a lot that can be done to make life better. You can explore ways through which you can manage your chronic pain and live with it. Below are some tips that can help you out.

Reduce stress:

Feelings like anxiety, stress and depression can elevate the pain and make you feel it more sharply. Reducing stress in your life can help you deal with chronic pain in a much better way. Do anything that lifts your mood and makes you feel great to reduce stress. Listen to music, read a book or talk to a friend who understands you.

Exercise more:

A lot of people with chronic pain assume that they do not

need to exercise as it will increase their pain. However, this is not true. You can consult your doctor about which type of exercise will be suitable for you and won't boost your pain. This way, you can keep your spirits high and feel motivated too. Exercise release endorphins in your body which are responsible for a great mood and positive vibes. Therefore, this can be extremely helpful in living with chronic pain.

Meditation:

Meditation helps your body relax and can be a wonderful way to deal with chronic pain too. Deep breathing is a great and easy way to meditate and allow the tension or stress to seep away from the muscles and out of your body. It is best to find a very quiet spot and sit alone, breathing deeply and feeling the pain leave your body or allowing any tension to be let go.

Decrease your alcohol intake:

Sleeping with chronic pain is tough, and if you drink alcohol, then it can just add up to the issue. Thus, decreasing your alcohol intake is important.

Join a support group:

You are not the only one dealing with chronic pain; a lot of people are facing the same issue. Joining a support group will help you realize that you are not alone in this, and you will get a platform to share your feelings. You will also find professionals in the group who can help you further in facing the situation.

Distract yourself:

Focusing on the pain is not going to help improve the situation; it will just worsen things. Thus, the best way to deal with it is to distract yourself. Find a hobby or do something that does not elevate the pain but also helps in distracting you from it. You need to find a way out of it, and distraction is going to help.

Stay positive:

This is easier said than done, but think of how many people out there who might be facing the same pain that you are. There is always something to be grateful about. Thus, look on the brighter side and talk to a professional about it and deal with it smartly.

To conclude it all, living with chronic pain is a struggle, but it is not impossible. You can deal with it wisely and distract yourself from the pain, too. It is a time-consuming process, but once you know how to handle it, it gets better. Stay positive and make sure that you follow a healthy diet and do not forget to exercise. Don't stress about it because it really won't help. Thus, stay happy and deal with it the way your professional doctor guides you to.

The Twilight Charity Walk 2019

"Creativity Is Intelligence Having Fun."

~Albert Einstein

CHAPTER 9
THE NHS CAREER

The National Healthcare Service is one of the biggest system set up for the residents of the UK. It is world renowned, and most individuals would be lucky to find a position with the NHS. However, before you decide for yourself, you should weigh your options for what would be a better fit: the NHS or a career in the private sector.

Choosing a career in the NHS is different for every person, and while there are many advantages, it is entirely dependent on the individual to decide if it is best suited for them.

Pros

Career development opportunities:

Working as a healthcare professional with the NHS allows you ample room to grow. They have a steady career ladder moving upwards, and even if you are starting fairly new, you will be given chances to rise to better positions. There are also pay raises with the new positions that you achieve. You will also receive mentors who will further help you in your career development.

Flexibility:

Since there are many NHS hospitals all over the country, you can get a lot more flexibility with your scheduling. You can choose the time that suits you best and pick a hospital that is closet to your home. Although you cannot pick and choose what you want specifically, they do allow a lot more room for their healthcare professionals to manage things more easily.

Cons

Pay rates:

The pay rates for the NHS are not bad by any means, and they do tend to offer a fair salary depending on your skills. These pay rates, however, are regulated and not as competitive with the salary packages the private sector offers for its health professionals. They did have a good pension package which drove people to them previously, though due to budget cuts the packages are not as appealing as they used to be.

Work environment:

The work environment in the NHS is usually extremely stressful and fast-paced. This is something that will take getting used to. The professionals have to deal with emergencies, and they have to make quick decisions. If that is something you are not capable of, you might want to look into private health care facilities.

I started my career with the NHS on the 20th of October 1991, working 37.5 hours each week. I worked different shift patterns; the early shift was from 07.00 a.m. to 03.00 p.m. and the late shift was from 03.00 p.m. to 09.00 p.m. I worked as a Mental Health Support Worker. My grandmother brought me up, so from a very young age I felt connected with elderly people. This was the reason why I wanted to care for people living with Dementia. I cared for both males and females for over 27 and a half years.

At the start of an early shift, the night staff would hand-over to the early staff regarding everything that had happened throughout the night. I would make bullet-point notes for my records. Then we would work in pairs or as a single, depending on the needs of our individual clients. For the more able clients, they were encouraged to do personal care independently, choose their own clothing for the day, do their hair and brush their teeth. It was convenient for them to do so because each bedroom had a sink. The client would be wheeled to the dining room in their wheelchair, where breakfast was served, assuming this client was able-bodied and also mobile.

If a client was not mobile and is also unable to give themselves personal care, then two staff members would need to assist with personal care and then transfer them into a wheelchair if they already used one. They would be wheeled to the dining room, where a member of staff would be in charge of serving breakfast. There were many different types of breakfast cereals, toast with varieties of butter and jam, plus porridge and cooked breakfast, which included scrambled eggs, sausages, bacon and tomatoes.

Some clients needed to be fed, while others needed encouragement before they would eat or drink. It was our duty to tick the list of clients who had eaten, so that nobody was forgotten. During breakfast, the trained nurse would give out medication and check on clients who were diabetic or had other medical conditions. After breakfast there would be activities with the Occupational Therapist and their assistants. Each activity was person centred, and would sometimes involve small groups of 4-6 clients, depending on their ability.

The most popular activities were singing and dancing. As an active member of a multi -disciplinary team, I assisted and engaged with the clients and organised and planned meaningful activities, and monitored clients' hygiene standards and ensured they were maintained throughout the day.

I had to ensure that I abided by the following:

- To participate in Cardio Pulmonary Resuscitation (CPR), Physical Intervention (PI), breakaway training and manual handling, and
- To be able to perform the required techniques as and when required.
- We had regular team meetings to contribute to clients' care review. Also to follow and demonstrate and implement care plans under the direction of a registered nurse.
- To provide privacy and dignity.
- To have zero tolerance of all forms of abuse. Meal times were protected and promoted as a social event.
- Play a role as an Allocated Key Worker, and accept responsibility for clients' everyday tasks. Accompany clients to other hospital appointments in an ambulance or in a taxi.
- To follow the code of practice and identify them.
- Adherence to national guidelines and best practice evidence on infection prevention and control.

When a client was admitted into our hospital, they usually arrived with a bag or suitcase, and we needed to make a record of each client's property and pass on any money or valuables to the Ward Clerk for storage. The bedrooms, wards, lounge and corridors had to be kept clean and tidy at all times. Laundry items had to be put back into clients' wardrobes, and we also had to make sure they were labelled.

If visitors made any complaints, we were to direct them to the nurse in charge of the shift. We were expected to always wear the correct uniform and understand the Health and Safety at Work Act, and a Food Hygiene Certificate had to be completed. We had to comply with the required training on the Deprivation of Liberty Safeguards and the Mental Health Act 2005.

Lunch was usually served after 12 noon, and a staff member would be allocated to the kitchen, and some staff would sit in the dining room with clients while others would be in the lounge area. Medications were given during meal times. There were three main course choices, including vegetarian, plus main hot and cold pudding, including cheese with biscuits, yoghurt and ice cream. After lunch was over, clients were assisted with personal care. Others that required bed rest were assisted to bed, especially if they had pressure areas or if it was part of their care plan. By 01.00 p.m. the afternoon staff would arrive at work, ready for their handover. There was always a member of staff in the lounge area doing general observation and head counts. Staff were expected to sit next to clients and engage in conversation with the client and their family.

Working with dementia patients was challenging, however it was an honour to support people through their most difficult times. It gave me a sense of gratitude when the clients' relatives visited and saw what we did for them.

Seeing and treating them as human beings and giving them that reassurance that their lives do matter and should be respected makes a world of a difference to them, as do providing dignity and showing empathy. Having human compassion, mind, heart, tolerance and patience all play a role in humanity.

Although people may not remember what you say or do, a

part of them will definitely remember how you made them feel. By making them feel valued, even if it's just for that moment, most certainly makes their day feel brighter with happiness and self-fulfilment. During the activities on the ward you could see a sparkle in their eyes. It was so rewarding to see that.

See them as more than people with illnesses, but merely just one of us

"Knowing Is Not Enough; We Must Apply. Wishing Is Not Enough; We Must Do."

~ Johann Wolfgang Von Goethe

CHAPTER 10
DEMENTIA

Dementia is a general term given to the disease associated with memory loss and the overall decline of the patient's ability to function. Dementia is when this memory loss becomes so severe to the point where the patient cannot perform everyday tasks.

Reasons for dementia

Dementia occurs when a person's brain cells are damaged. This can be one brain cell which is then unable to communicate with other brain cells. This, in turn, leads to changes in the person's ability to think, talk and feel.

The most common reason for dementia is a stroke. This is more commonly known as vascular dementia. Alzheimer's disease accounts for 70 to 80 per cent of patients diagnosed with dementia. Some cases of dementia are even reversible, such as those caused by thyroid issues or vitamin deficiencies.

Symptoms of dementia

Depending on what part of the brain is affected, dementia can have varying symptoms in different people. However, some core features must be greatly impaired for it to be considered dementia. These include memory loss, being unable to communicate, an inability to focus, and a lack of perception or lack of judgement to make decisions.

Types of dementia

- Alzheimer's disease: The most common type of dementia and are likely to occur in older people typically 40 to 50 years old.
- Vascular dementia: Caused by a lack of blood flow to the brain.
- Dementia with Lewy bodies: Due to protein deposits in the nerves which restrict the chemical messages.
- Parkinson's disease: People with advanced Parkinson's disease are likely to develop dementia, and they can have trouble doing simple tasks.
- Frontotemporal dementia: Used to describe different forms of dementia which affect the front and the side of the brain, also known as Pick's disease.

Other types of dementia include:

- Creutzfeldt-Jakob disease
- Mixed dementia
- Wernicke-Korsakoff syndrome
- Huntington's disease
- Normal pressure hydrocephalus

Bournemouth, Dorset, is the UK capital of dementia, with the highest rate of patients with dementia. I am on a mission to set up a worldwide charity for dementia patients. My vision of the charity is to have a day care centre that can provide clients with activities they are able to do. Give the careers a break from time to time. We would provide a service where a mini bus would pick them up directly from their homes and look after them for the rest of the day. Only 5% of nursing homes in the UK do activities with their clients. This is my purpose, vision and mission in life, to set a legacy where I am able to help as many people achieve this as possible. I want to connect the charity worldwide, making it a global project.

Life is like a flower it will wilt when not looked after but blossom with its full potential when it is....

In Bournemouth…..

Life is better with sand
between our toes....

CHAPTER 11
MY LIFE TODAY

Hands up I can say today that I am one of the happiest women I know. Having gone through so many challenges in life the past couple of months had been life changing.

My life has changed in just 9 months, since I said "Yes" to an invitation to a meeting in London. I have been able to speak at events in London, made amazing friends, and have also written a book.

"I know the Lord is always with me, I will not be shaken, for He is right beside me"
~ PSALM 16:8.

I love this verse in the Bible. King David discovers that joy is far deeper than happiness. Joy can be felt even in the midst of and in spite of one's deepest troubles. Happiness is temporary because it is based on external circumstances, but joy is lasting because it is based on God's presence with us. As we learn to contemplate this presence, not only will we grow in contentment, we will also discover the deeper joy that is connected to our confidence in God's abiding love for us.

Last year in February, 2018, on a bright sunny afternoon, I walked up the road to get some soya milk and bread. As I entered Tesco, a lady approached me to ask where I had bought the colourful dress that I was wearing. She said, "I am sure you didn't buy that dress from New Look", and we both smiled at the statement. I finished buying the few items I wanted and we both stood outside the shop and continued our conversation. After we finished talking, she offered me her mobile number. The funny thing about that particular day I met Sarah Sheppard: She has a local Tesco shop near her house, but chose to visit the one local to me, instead.

I decided to contact Sarah after 2 months to touch base, and she replied immediately. This was in April by then. We kept in touch, and then on the 13th of September, just after 1p.m., I received several short text messages from Sarah, asking me for my email address which I texted back to her. Her reply was "Please keep the 19th and 30th of September free, we are needed in London. Now the 19th is a fantastic event. Please prepare a very short pitch about yourself including wanting to speak and inspire-you will be mixing with millionaires and lots of business people, so wear something smart and lovely from your fab wardrobe. Philip has put us on his guest list so we don't have to pay £107 to attend, and the 30th again is free. I will book your ticket so it's ready". I replied back to her, saying, "I would like to thank you very much".

On Wednesday the 19th of September, Sarah sent me all the information, including the address where the Intelligent Millionaire Network Event, "IMN", was going to take place. Even though I was looking forward to my coach journey to London Victoria Coach Station, I was nervous at the same time, as didn't know what to expect. I travelled on my own. My new friend offered to buy my ticket online, as I had never bought tickets online before and find technology challenging, to say the least. I arrived safely at the coach station, went to top-up my Oyster Card, and then boarded the Underground Victoria Line, which took me to Euston Station. It was a very busy afternoon, at around 4p.m, with lots of people going about doing their own stuff. The night before, my partner and daughter had given me directions to the hotel. Only less than 5 minutes' walk for me. When I arrived, Sarah was waiting for me. She introduced me to Phillip Chan, and we both shook hands and chatted. I met two film directors, a female model, a few business men, and we exchanged business cards. Everything was flowing well. Then Sarah told me that she is a model and hadn't wanted to share that information with me when we met in Tesco in February. We talked for several minutes. We started taking photos with different people, and by that time I was feeling more relaxed. Then lots of people started arriving. Cold and hot drinks were on different tables for self-service.

We were told to go into a room where there were chairs in rows, leaving a space in the middle for people to walk. I listened to the first speaker, had a 15 minutes break, and talked to more people. I was so surprised that everyone was so friendly. I told people that I am a single mother who has raised two kids on my own, so I wanted to be a motivational speaker for single parents. The event was lots of fun. I travelled back to Victoria to get my coach to Bournemouth. I was very tired and was in lots of pain, but I never talked about it with anyone.

I decided to join IMN a few weeks later. I received an email from the owners of IMN telling me to prepare a few-minute testimonial speech which I would give at their Bonus Event on Monday the 1st of October. I felt nervous and managed to write few bullet-points on a piece of A4 paper.

I travelled to Victoria Coach station and got the underground again to the Millennium Gloucester Hotel London. There were four people giving testimonials that evening, three ladies and 1 man. When my name was called, I cannot tell you how my stomach felt at that moment, the nerves with everything else going on in my head. I had my A4 paper in my hand, and I was the first to give my testimonial. After the first minute I was less anxious and my speech flowed well, and my confidence came back to me. A lady sitting next to me recorded me, and we became friends and exchanged mobile numbers. She sent the video of my speech to me, and on my return journey home I watched myself and sent the video to my children and partner. It was a fun evening, and I loved what I felt that evening. I never would have imagined I could stand in a room full of people and give a speech. I thought surely it would get easier the more I do it. Philip Chang and I became friends, and I kept regular contact with all the people that gave me their business cards. Keeping in touch with people is almost second nature to me, as I had many pen-pals while I was in boarding school. I loved writing letters to people across the world. During this event we were told that there was going to be Mega Success event in LA in the USA. As my son was already studying at California State University of Long beach (Cal State), I was thinking of visiting him in November. I could not believe the coincidence. I believed it was all part of God's plan for me. My chronic pain continued, but it was nice to have this distraction.

I arrived at LA again, since I had already been there in August, just over 9 weeks before when I was visiting my second cousin. I bought a ticket for the event for my son and his friend. They joined me in the late afternoon when they finished their classes at university. Mega Success was a massive event in LA. I had never been in a building that large; it could hold more than two and a half thousand people. I felt shy for a moment or two, and then started chatting with a few people. I talked with some of the IMN members I already knew from London. It was an incredible experience to listen to hundreds of speakers, and be in the same room with top Hollywood actors, actresses, musicians, billionaires, millionaires, and entrepreneurs. Every walk of life one could ever imagine was in that massive hall. I spent 10 days in LA with my son, it was nice to see him settling in at university and making new friendships. He was enjoying the student life, visiting places like Disney and Warner Brothers Studios, experiencing his life as an animator. This has been his life-long vision ever since he was two and a half years old, when he started watching Sonic, one of his favourite cartoon characters. I am so proud of you, my son, for being so brave and wanting to go all the way to California to learn to live an independent life on your own. Regardless of all the challenges you faced, you kept going, because you want to be an animator, by the Grace of our Almighty Father. Thank you Lord for guiding me and my children all these years, for protecting us, supporting us, providing for us, caring for us, loving us and most of all for your Grace and Mercy in our lives.

With Philip Chan

It has been just over 9 months since I was invited by Philip Chan to attend the IMN event in London. I am living with this chronic pain in my body 24 hours a day, and taking medication which does not help with my pain. But I try to stay positive each day, as I learnt as a very young child to show gratitude, and to make the most of each day and count my blessings instead of complaining. This attitude has helped me throughout my life. I am grateful to have survived 2 major open surgeries within 9 months, also considering all the complications that happened, which has left me learning to live my life with this chronic pain I endure each blessed day, 24 hours a day. The pain I experience is like labour pain. I can hardly move. I have written an autobiography about my life and want to encourage people no matter what they may be going through. You should try to be grateful for all the other things that you have in your life, and keep a positive mind. You will have down days and up days, which is all part of life. Bad things will always happen in our lives, because we are human and none of us is perfect. So let's try and be happy and joyful for our family and friends we have in our lives. All I did was say "Yes" to a complete stranger in a Tesco Supermarket, and I am now an "author. Who would have thought the girl next door from the East End of Freetown, Sierra Leone, would publish a book in England, and that people across the whole wide world would be reading this book!?

In the summer of 2016 my son was preparing to leave home to go and further his education at university in the Midlands. A week before he was due to leave home, I ended up with a massive gout attack. This big move meant that my son, daughter and I had more than four cases with several bags in order to escort my son to his university accommodations. Due to the gout I could not wear full shoes, as the gout was on my right big toe, which meant I had to wear flip-flops. I was comfortable with my flip-flops but was worried about my painful gout toe. We settled my son at university and then I returned back home with my daughter.

I started to experience anxiety. I had lots of restless nights, worrying about how my son was going to cope with university life with his special needs. He was in a new environment, with lots of different routines, away from home and familiar surroundings, family, friends, and comfort zones. Even though my son was keeping in touch regularly, I could not stop worrying. So I decided to visit him every 3 weeks, just to help him settle in with his new environment. My anxiety continued, and have learnt to deal with it on my own, because I am a confident, strong and positive lady, and this has helped me in so many ways without realising it. This chronic pain gets to me sometimes and I feel fed-up and tired of being strong all the time, because people assume that because I am always smiling , and have a big green on my face, I don't complain or grumble about things. I am just an ordinary woman and God is bigger than any problems. I thank God each day I get through, regardless of my circumstances.

With my partner with whom I've been with for 6 years and as happier as ever.

Awards I received because of my vocation and caring for
people living with Dementia.

Printed in Poland
by Amazon Fulfillment
Poland Sp. z o.o., Wrocław